Puppies

by Judith E. Rinard
Photographs by Joseph H. Bailey

A golden retriever puppy gives his owner a friendly lick.

☐ BOOKS FOR YOUNG EXPLORERS
☐ NATIONAL GEOGRAPHIC SOCIETY

Seven furry puppies snuggle close to their mother. They drink her milk. The puppies are two weeks old. Young puppies need their mother.

She feeds them and cleans them. She keeps them safe and warm.

GOLDEN RETRIEVERS

These puppies are a day old. They cannot see or hear. Their eyes and ears are closed. Their legs are wobbly.

The puppies sleep awhile. Then they find their mother's nipples so they can nurse. What a lot of hungry puppies! How many can you count?

MASTIFF PUPPIES

Puppies grow very quickly. Their eyes open. They can hear. A Dalmatian puppy chews a toy. Mastiff puppies play with an older dog. Beagles tug on a slipper.

These retrievers are playful, too.
They nip and chase and jump at
each other, over and over again.

Sniff, sniff! Two beagle puppies explore the yard. They are excited, and their tails are wagging fast. Puppies spend a lot of time exploring. They are curious about everything around them.

When puppies are eight weeks old, they are ready to leave their mothers. Now they can become good pets.

They are very friendly and playful. They like to be with people. Which of these puppies would you choose?

A visit to a dog show can help you decide what kind of puppy you want. The boy and his mother are holding two Dalmatians that were advertised in the newspaper. They may buy one.

You can buy a puppy
from a breeder who
raises puppies to sell.

Valerie pets two beagles
through a fence. She
finally chooses a puppy
to take home with her.

Melissa can't decide which
retriever puppy she wants.
Sometimes it's hard to choose.

When Melissa brings her new puppy home, she takes good care of it. She puts her pet in a warm, cozy basket to sleep. She named her puppy Sandy. Good night, Sandy!

Bryan learns to feed his puppy, Kip. He gives her fresh food and plenty of water in clean bowls.

Puppies often need grooming.
Kip got wet playing outside.
Bryan helps dry her off
and fluff up her coat.
He likes grooming Kip.

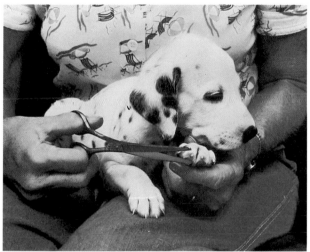

This Dalmatian has long nails.
They grew fast. Now the puppy
is having its nails trimmed.

Valerie grooms her beagle
with a brush. Brushing removes
loose hair. It also helps keep
the puppy's coat shiny and
clean. The puppy likes it.

Playtime! Bryan and Steven wrestle in the yard, and Kip joins right in. She tugs at Bryan as he tumbles over Steven. Puppies like to romp and play with people.

Kip chases the boys and plays games with them. Playing is good exercise for her. It helps keep her healthy and strong.

These puppies are being trained. A boy teaches his retriever to HEEL, or walk by his side. Then he teaches her to SIT.

Mr. Nagler, the trainer, uses his hands to tell a Dalmatian to STAY.

A white terrier learns
to retrieve a ball.
"Get it, Jody! Get it!"
When Jody brings
the ball back, the boy
says, "Good dog!"

Peter is training his puppy, Charlie, to ride in the car. First, he walks Charlie to the car and helps him get in. Then he tells Charlie to SIT on the front seat and STAY. When Charlie obeys, Peter says, "Good dog!" Charlie will learn not to jump from seat to seat or from side to side.

Peter and his father take Charlie to a veterinarian for a checkup. The doctor tests Charlie's heart and lungs to make sure they are healthy.

Then he looks at Charlie's eyes and ears. Next, the veterinarian will give Charlie shots to protect him against diseases.

Puppies are frisky. Kip grabs the hose for a game of tug-of-war. Then she chases a ball. Bryan and Steven play with Kip every day.

They like taking care of her and watching her grow. Soon she will be a big dog, but she will always need them to look after her.

What fun Steven and Kip are having!
Puppies like being wherever you are.
They need you, and they want to please you.
Best of all, puppies are warm friends.

A sleepy puppy rests on Melissa's shoulder. The puppy is 16 days old. Puppies must have love and care.

Published by The National Geographic Society
Gilbert M. Grosvenor, *President;* Melvin M. Payne,
Chairman of the Board; Owen R. Anderson, *Executive
Vice President;* Robert L. Breeden, *Vice President,
Publications and Educational Media*

Prepared by The Special Publications Division
Donald J. Crump, *Director*
Philip B. Silcott, *Associate Director*
William L. Allen, William R. Gray, *Assistant Directors*

Staff for this Book
Margery G. Dunn, *Managing Editor*
Jim Abercrombie, *Picture Editor*
Cinda Rose, *Art Director*
Peggy D. Winston, *Researcher*
Katheryn M. Slocum, *Illustrations Assistant*

Engraving, Printing, and Product Manufacture
Robert W. Messer, *Manager*
George V. White, *Production Manager*
David V. Showers, *Production Project Manager*
Mark R. Dunlevy, Richard A. McClure, Raja D. Murshed,
   Gregory Storer, *Assistant Production Managers*
Katherine H. Donohue, *Senior Production Assistant*
Katherine R. Leitch, *Production Staff Assistant*
Nancy F. Berry, Pamela A. Black, Nettie Burke,
   Claire M. Doig, Rosamund Garner, Victoria D. Garrett,
   Sheryl A. Hoey, Virginia A. McCoy, Cleo Petroff,
   Victoria I. Piscopo, Tammy Presley, Carol A. Rocheleau,
   Jenny Takacs, *Staff Assistants*

Consultants
Dr. Glenn O. Blough, Judith Hobart, *Educational Consultants*
Lynda Ehrlich, *Reading Consultant*

The Special Publications Division is grateful to those
cited here for their generous assistance in the preparation
of this book: Kenneth M. Nagler, Bespeckled Kennels,
Hyattsville, Maryland (Dalmatians); Lois Purnell (golden
retrievers); Toni Cisneros, Night Stalkers Kennels, Annapolis,
Maryland (mastiffs); George Lerch, Stonehall Kennels,
Beltsville, Maryland (beagles); Cade Beach;
Michelle Downs; and United Breeders' Association.

Library of Congress CIP Data

Rinard, Judith E.
   Puppies.

   (Books for young explorers)
   Summary: Text and photos highlight the care of puppies by their mothers and their subsequent
   selection, training, and care as pets.
   1. Puppies—Juvenile literature. 2. Dog breeds—Juvenile literature. [1. Dogs] I. Bailey, Joseph H.,
   ill. II. Title. III. Series.
   SF426.5.R56   636.7'07   82-47857
   ISBN 0-87044-451-4 (library binding)   AACR2

COVER: Five-week-old Dalmatians snuggle together on a rug. Very young puppies sleep much of the time.